ALASKA ABC Book

By Charlene Kreeger and Shannon Cartwright

Drawings by Shannon Cartwright

Printed on recycled paper

Copyright 1978 by Charlene Kreeger and Shannon Cartwright

15 17 19 21 20 18 16 14

ISBN 0-934007-17-9 (hc)
ISBN 0-933914-01-6 (pb)

Library of Congress Number 86-60735

Alaska ABC Book
Box 2364
Homer, Alaska 99603

To Madison,
Hi from the
Polar Bear in a Parka!
Shannon Cartwright
1996

Alaska and

animals

Bear and a bucket of berries

Caribou covering a cabin

Dd Dall sheep going down

E e

Eskimo and eagle eating

F f

Fox and forget-me-nots

Goats gliding down a glacier

Huskies hauling a halibut

Iceworm in an igloo

Just jade

King crab in a kayak

Lynx on a log

Moose in mukluks

Northern lights at night

Otter in the ocean

Polar bear in a parka

Qiviut and quills

Reindeer in the rain

Salmon snowshoeing

Two tall totem poles

Using ulus

Vegetables in the valley

Whale watering a walrus

eXtra large state

Yy

Yukon River

Zero temperatures

32°F   0°C

zzzzzzz z Z Z Z

Glossary

We knew there would be a few "funny" words that might be hard to understand so we have provided an explanation here.

Forget-me-nots - not really a funny word, but we want you to know that this lovely flower is the state flower of Alaska.

Qiviut - This is a soft, fluffy wool found in the undercoat of the musk ox.

The yarn is distributed to Eskimos in many Arctic villages. The women knit the wool into very soft scarves and hats.

Ulus - This is the name given the knives which the Eskimos use to skin whale and other animals.

Vegetables - There is a valley in Alaska called the Matanuska valley where very large vegetables are grown. Giant cabbages sometimes weigh as much as 72 pounds. Turnips may weigh as much as 40 pounds. This is due to the long hours of sunlight in the summer.

Yukon River - This is the longest river in Alaska.

Other titles from PAWS IV PUBLISHING COMPANY

The ALASKA MOTHER GOOSE

THUNDERFEET

KIANA'S IDITAROD

ALASKA'S THREE BEARS

MAMMOTH MAGIC

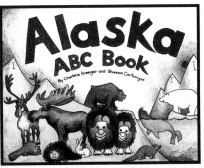

The ALASKA ABC BOOK

DANGER-The dog yard cat

PAWS IV PUBLISHING
BOX 2364
HOMER, ALASKA 99603